Because You Were Chosen

– A Memoir –

Ivory Bennett

Copyright © 2016 by Ivory Bennett

All rights reserved. No part of this publication may be reproduced, distributed, or broadcasted in any form or by any means, including photocopying, recording, or other electronic or mechanical methods, without the prior written permission of the publisher, except in the case of brief quotations embodied in critical reviews and certain other noncommercial uses permitted by copyright law. For permission requests, please contact the publisher at:

GriotteGoddess@gmail.com

Ordering Information:

Special discounts are available on quantity purchases by corporations, associations, and others. For details, contact the author using the contact information above.

Printed in the United States of America.

Second Edition

First Printing, 2018

ISBN: 978-0-578-19677-0

www.GriotteGoddess.com

Cover Design by Ivory Bennett
Cover Art by Ivory Bennett

Contents

Chapter 1	*4*
Chapter 2	*7*
Chapter 3	*13*
Chapter 4	*20*
Chapter 5	*27*
Chapter 6	*33*
Chapter 7	*39*
Chapter 8	*46*

Because You Were Chosen

– A Memoir –

Ivory Bennett

"She told me about a group of people in Guinea who carry the sky on their heads. They are people of Creation. Strong, tall, and mighty people who can bear anything. Their maker, she said, gives them the sky to carry because they are strong. These people do not know who they are, but if you see a lot of trouble in your life, it is because you were chosen to carry part of the sky on your head."

- Edwidge Danticat, "*Breath, Eyes, Memory.*"

Chapter 1

"I love you. Every part of you. You are a part of me – from the tips of your toes to the end of every kinky curl. My twin."

"Why did you name me Ivory?"

"You want to know why? Ivory. Do you know that Ivory is rare? A rare and precious gift. And strong – almost unbreakable. People will spend a lot of time and resources to find you. To hold you. To have you – even just a tiny little piece of you.

You are expensive – only the best should have access to your light. And those who are living in darkness will be drawn to you for that very reason.

Ivory.
Ivory is pure. It is – you are –

balanced. Just as the beginning and the end of time meet to reconcile – so will the work you must do in this world.

You were chosen to be my child. You were chosen to be a part of me. I thank God for your beauty. I thank God for your strength...

Sing me a song.

Please."

Chapter 2

Is it possible to be deeply in love with the memory of someone? I wondered. Even after you realize that person – those moments – are gone forever?

Forever.

The sound of the respirator collided with the sound of the heart monitor in my mother's room.

Cacophony.

Suddenly, I became aware of the cold sweat beads clinging to my back. I was wearing a black leotard that exposed my skin. But, I still felt hot. My muscles were tense from the dancing in my West African dance class and from the uncertainty of my mother's fate.

I received the initial call in my vocal musicianship class. I loved to sing. Recently, I decided to minor in Theatre with a focus on acting. This vocal class was a requirement – and I could only miss so many days before I would fail.

Even at my mother's bedside, I felt alone. She was unconscious. She had fallen down a flight of stairs and had broken her neck. Workers at the group home said she had a seizure on the flight of stairs. Doctors said her seizure was caused by a cocktail of psychotropic drugs.

Not even her eyes were moving. She couldn't breathe on her own. Her spinal cord was being held together by a metal rod at the nape of her neck.
And *my* heart was broken.

I wished they made a metal contraption that could hold me together in times like these – times when you feel scattered, like an old, worn cloth abandoned and bouncing in the breeze. Times, when the wetness of tears is the only thing that lets you know you are still alive. You're still here, held together by destiny, searching for the purpose in your pain – your fingers, swimming in shallow pools, scraping floors with pillowy finger tips, almond nails fumbling for something that you can hold onto and make sense of, tapping the crevices of wood and granite, finally gripping hold of something, anything, so that you can anchor yourself, take a deep breath and find the courage to try once more, even if only for a little while.

    I grabbed my mother's hand and held onto it. It was almost as if I was guiding her across a busy intersection and I didn't want her to lose hold of me. Gently, I rubbed my thumb across her deep nail beds. I would paint them pink when I came back again.

    "Miss Bennett, can I speak with you a moment?"

Miss? I was only 20 years old, I thought to myself. Without looking towards the curtains that blocked out the rest of the ICU and all of the tragedy it contained, like an extra large Ziploc baggie.

"Sure."

I didn't want to let go of her hand. I couldn't. What if something else happened?

"Can we speak here?"

"Yes. As you know, your mother is in grave condition. We were able to stabilize her neck using the rod. More surgeries will be required, if the situation permits. But, for now, we need your signature to administer all life-sustaining medications. It's been a little while now. And you, as power of attorney, have to decide to sustain her life support."

"You were chosen to be my child,"

I thought to myself. These words sprinted in circles in my thoughts and danced to the drum of the machines connected to my mother's body.

So desperately, I wanted her to ask, "Sing me a song."

Please.

Chapter 3

"God does not send the illness. God is the creator of beautiful things. Illness is sent by the spirits of our ancestors when we don't honor them as we should."
- Sergio G. Sánchez, *Palm Trees in the Snow*

What do you do when an illness lives inside of you, beautiful thing? What have I done to dishonor the ancestors? Please, forgive me. Forgive us, for we know not what we've done.

I remember feeling so betrayed by God. How could He let this happen – Type 1 Diabetes? And I didn't blame Him – He didn't make me sick. But, He allowed it. Isn't it just as bad when you idly stand by and allow something to happen to someone you love? I felt everything but seen or known. I felt that I needed protection from someone who promised to never leave me or forsake me... but was willing to watch me suffer. He watched me hurt. And I couldn't make sense of it. I still haven't, quite yet.

"You think your life is hard because you have to buy yourself insulin? Because you have to spend an extra year in college? Big whoop!"

My mother looked at me with piercing eyes. This was not her. This woman in front of me was someone else. My mother was kind. This woman was cruel – she knew how to cut you with her words.

I placed her fork gently back onto her tray. She was nearly done with her dinner, anyways.

"Goodbye, Mom. I love you. I'll ask the nurses to help you finish your drink and dessert."

She began to frantically cry. I didn't look back. The hospital door clicked as I exited. I took a deep breath. And the lump in the back of my throat returned from where it came.

She wasn't always this angry. She wasn't always so full of hate and hurt. I remember, she taught us to always love, always be kind. Treat others, as you would want to be treated. Being paralyzed hardened her from the inside out.

I should have let her die. Maybe, I made the wrong decision.

No one can tell you how to successfully be the child of a mentally ill parent. Too often, people don't realize that we endure their sickness with them. There aren't steps to follow for a fruitful outcome. Something that works at one point in time, won't work in another. It's hit or miss, in the most painful way. And if you manage to somehow heal the wounds of your endurance. One word. One disagreement. One tiny mishap can rip your flesh open again to pain, only each time it takes longer to heal because you've already been broken. It's no wonder that you fear. It's no wonder that you don't feel safe in love.

Sometimes, I think of my parents as keloids. They disrupt my beauty, the continuity of my nature. And yet, they make me more unique and authentic – they make me more me. Their ridges add height and depth to places that are plains in other people. These scars – my parents – remind me that life is always repairing itself, even until death. There's magic in that. The ability to grow, again and again and again. In spite. And no matter how much a wound is hacked into, time and time again – it will heal. You will strengthen.

It is beyond hard to be the child of a parent who suffers from extreme mental illness – the experience is truly unlike any other. Moments can go from magical to maniacal, in the blink of an eye. This experience has showed me, that at the end of the day, no one – regardless of mental stability – wants to be alone in his or her suffering. People will do whatever it takes – the good, the bad, the ugly, subconsciously, consciously, and unconsciously – to not feel alone in their emotional states of being.

And, at the end of the day, parent or not, you have to set boundaries. No one has the right to hurt you in any capacity, for any reason, under any circumstances.

Learn from those who hurt you,
In that wisdom lies your healing.
Learn from those who love you,
In that wisdom lies your strength.

Chapter 4

God's Child

Realizing who and what I am really feels quite fine.
Knowing that I am truly unique and blessed by God divine.
He picked me out as He felt He should, not of goodness of my own.
Said, I have a mission for you to complete, and I will never leave you alone.
I want you to touch the hearts of man and help them plainly see,
That I am God omnipotent and your power - it comes from me.
Your faith, your strength, your love, your power and everything within – if you use it for my purpose, I will finish all that you do begin.
Your fears and your tears when the way seems rough and you just don't

understand —

It will melt like pearl drops of quick silver in your hand.

And all the things you do for me, I will not see in vain.

For I am the King and will always be.

No other King shall reign.

And when your story's over, you shall wear a starry crown. And for each star placed there by faith, believing I would never let you down,

I'm going to add another star and cause it brightly so to shine. So that no matter, where 'ere you may be, all existence will know you are mine.

- Constance Bennett

The little girl across the street holding her mother's hand unsteadily reminded me of my own childhood. A place where the world was my mother's stage. Countless times, Ebony and I, we found ourselves impatiently at our mother's side while she performed for strangers – people she smiled at while walking down the street or an old friend from some elusive part of her past.

You see, my mother was a storyteller. A generous griotte goddess and a healer of hearts. A soul whose spirit drifted in and out of this earthly realm far too often to keep up with it.

Sometimes, these performances, or more accurately, summoning of souls, would end in teary prayers of shouting and salvation. Often, she ushered faith and hope into the hearts of people who didn't even realize they were missing something. Her words fell like cleansing waters.

I knew all of her poems by heart. I knew the influxes of her voice, the cadence of her cries, the timing of her tone, the rhythm of the wind she gathered in her lungs to bellow the psalms of her spirit to anyone who would listen.

Everywhere we travelled we accrued new aunties, cousins, and siblings - my mother was a lover of people.

People.

Hurt people hurt people.

I always have to remind myself of that, as silly as it may sound.

And family.

What does that really mean? Should family be able to hurt you again and again and again? Just because they are... Family.

I wasn't sure.

However, I was sure that my family was full of hurt people. Hurt people who were afraid and uncertain. Hurt people, who somewhere along the way, inherited pain and made it a permanent fixture in our legacy.

And what a legacy it was. Uncles were like fathers. Cousins were like siblings. Aunts were like mothers. Siblings were like enemies. Mothers were like friends. Fathers were... unfamiliar.

"How did I even get here," I wondered as I read through the course catalogue. I would have to spend another year completing my degree because I failed nearly every class the semester that my mother almost died.

Where was family, then?

Chapter 5

"Women are the water of the revolution."
- April Fool Child

    Perhaps, that is why we hold in our tears. We are the keepers of the floods. Guarding our children and our lovers from the unkindness, unholiness of the world. Only, sometimes, our children and our lovers look past us and we become invisible. Necessary, but invisible. And our love is too true, too steadfast to abandon at the whim of a bruised and broken ego.

    So, we push past the pain. And sometimes we fall.

    We fall, crashing into the pieces of ourselves that are free and unoccupied with service to others. All the while, holding back those waters for fear of flooding our villages with the hatred of those who don't see, won't see, can't see our beauty or even care.

I see it. I watch it permeate the ripples of those midnight waves that come crashing onto self. I see my reflection in yours. My melanin is a mahogany map of my past, our present, and their future.

I feel it. When I reach out to hug you, only to feel pieces of your soul slip through my fingertips back into the pools of our people. My people.

Rarely, I saw my Nana cry. My mother cried often and for any reason – sometimes, no reason at all. My sister cried enough for the both of us. I don't know who taught me or where I even learned it – but, I did not cry. My crying was silent. An inward suffering that lasted way longer than the rows of tears on my dear sister's cheek. My silent cries carried me into an adulthood of fearfulness surrounding my ability to break – fearfulness of my own waters.

My inability to cry – to feel pain as it happened, as one should – was worn on my shoulders as a badge of honor. A burden I immediately hoisted onto the bridge of my back. Yes, it hurt – I hurt. I cried, in theory – my quietness, my disconnectedness from the trauma and the pain of an arduous childhood warranted way more than tears. Still, I could not gift myself the cleansing waters of shed sorrows. Out of reverence to my ego, I stood by the shore of my river, in wait.

However, there came a day when the dam of my emotions swelled too full. I had to make a choice. I could liberate my humanity and feel all of the things that threatened my freedom. Or, I could drown in a torrential down pouring of my pain.

    I chose change. I chose waters and revolution.

    Warm are the waters of self-reverence – all change, good or bad, is a choice. Sometimes, these rivers carry us to wondrous places. Other times, these rivers drown us unexpectedly. We are taught, from a young age, that these waterways were carved from the flowing of our ancestors to protect us; it is full of the love and hope of those who have come before us. We are taught that our ancestors guide its current with the wisdom of the cosmos. We are also taught to fear these rivers – for, it is tradition. We are taught to wade these waters, withholding any questions – thus, leaving them for collection along the shore.

I ask why.

Why did I fear these rivers? How and when did these waters become more threatening, more stifling than the silencing of my own suffering?

As a child, I had not arrived at the basin of burdens – the place where the waters of the world meet and our collective struggles connect. As a child, I was unaware of the tributaries of trial, the epochs of estuaries. Places where everyone must visit and collect its waters in their gourds.

As a child, time had not carried me far enough into the sea of sorrows to drown and devour my soul and its memories of present and past lives – its memory of strength and survival.

Chapter 6

My memory is sketchy. I rarely remember names. I suppose some may see that as careless or rude – it's not personal. As a child, I was never anywhere long enough to need to recall someone's name. And the names that I did know, I carried with me in the tapestries of my heart.

To my knowledge, I attended about twelve schools. I lived in about the same amount of foster homes, give or take a few, kinship care placements, and one shelter.

What's a name when you sleep in a bed that smells of someone else? What's a name when you have no artifacts of your own childhood? What's a name to me when I'm constantly moving to another new place full of temporary faces?

Toni Morrison once said, "All water

has a perfect memory and is forever trying to get back to where it was." Where was I? And where was my perfect memory? Perhaps, mine existed in sound – I can remember someone's voice just by hearing it once. Maybe my memory was sound and song. Music.

Maybe, memory is geographic. I see pain in the hills. And joy in the valleys. Rivers flow of my tears. Paths remind me of years.

Here, under this tree lies laughter. Under that bridge, surprise. Fear rest on that cliff, yonder. The future floats along those tree lines in the foggy distance. So, where does that leave me now? Better yet, where was my mother? Does she remember all the people she has ever been? My God, all of the mothers I have had. And is she, in all her different personalities, attempting to return to the same place?

I used to think she had somehow gotten lost in the darkness of her sadness. Other times, it seemed to me, that she got lost in the light of a world that was real to only her.

"My mother has bi-polar disorder," I would tell the court people when they asked if I knew why I was, wherever I was. Before I could tie my shoes or spell my middle name, I knew about bi-polar disorder, schizophrenia, and paranoia. I knew about having nothing. I knew about the insides of psych wards and the seriousness of medications – never to be played with for fear of contagion. I knew about empty eyes and hardened hearts. I knew about death before I knew about life.

When you have nothing to share but yourself, that's when one of two things happens: you become a tree of knowledge that keeps growing and providing for all of those around it or you lose the roots of yourself to silence and drift away.

    My mother taught me a few key things that are with me always. They are my anchors, my roots: never litter, share everything that you have, you are beautiful and talented and worthy – therefore, love yourself in all ways, always.

    Usually, when a child hears, "you're so much like your mother," that child may wander into the future, annoyed that he or she could have any of the same traits as the woman who birthed him or her. Sometimes, an eye roll or a suck of the teeth would indicate a displeasure at the flowering of such similarities. Usually, it's not such a horribly terrifying, unspeakable thing to hear. However, such a phrase carries a different meaning to children of the severely mentally ill – I am not sick like her... Or, am I? Paranoia and paralyzation accompany such a statement when made to said subjects. Comparisons, even the most well meaning, evoked – evoke – terror and fear in my heart. I love my mother – but I am not just like her. I am me. And she is many. And we are not – cannot be – the same.

Chapter 7

Where is the little girl in you? Where is she hiding? Does she have a voice? Does she play in the solitude of the sun? Where is she? Ivory. Ivory!

I... I don't know. Had I ever known her? Does she know me?

I know what it feels like to have someone look at you and not believe in you because of the color of your skin. The magnitude of my melanin magic was invisible to certain people – and I could always see that in their eyes... Their unwillingness to invest time and energy into your gifts, your spirit. Their apprehension when interacting with you to avoid getting too close to your actual humanity.

We must think of children as empty toolboxes. It is our obligation as elders to fill their boxes – their minds and their hearts with the endless possibilities of love. Of hope and compassion. A willingness and desire to listen, to grow. Strength to challenge injustice. The courage to make mistakes and to continue the pursuit of understanding. Wisdom and all of the peace that accompanies such.

I often ask myself, "why did anyone let my mother have children?"

We have suffered so much. We didn't ask to be here. My mother told me that I was made out of love - little does she know how much that enraged me. So, because you felt passionate, that was enough of a reason to bring life into your world of dysfunction? When is the last time your love met my needs? Your love didn't protect me from all the pain you caused me.

I, we, would have been better off unborn. My older sister has anorexia and probably obsessive-compulsive disorder with a fixation on money and cleanliness. She is starving my nephew, which has delayed his development. She won't let us see him. And I can only hope that he knows how much we love him. My little sister told me that she smokes marijuana everyday to keep from crying. Did you know that we have PTSD?

There was a moment, in the basement of a foster home. We were playing and she told me that someone violated her, in the worst way. She was maybe five. You brought him into our lives. And I told her she was lying because the pain of me not protecting her was too much of a burden on my soul. But, I knew the truth because he had violated me, too.

Every few days Ebony goes to

visit you, brings you food, and braids your hair. In return, you gift her sadness, in one way or another, and you rarely notice the pain you've caused. Where is the love in that, Mommy?

I think it's selfish to bring forth lives that you cannot afford. It's selfish to bring forth life that you cannot fight for, nurture or protect – for whatever reason.

Unbeknownst to her, much like most parents, she has passed down habits that are hard to release. And unlike other parents who pass down low self-esteem or racism, my mother passed down the habits of her mental illness. My sister and I, we dwell in dimly lit spaces. For me, personally, highly emotional people trigger me negatively. I don't trust, or even like people who immediately act on their emotions. I'm attracted to men who are fantastical – all talk and no actualization. Pretty men with pretty words who are, simply stated, empty. One of my biggest fears is having a child who is just like my mother. I'm not sure that I could deal with that, at all.

The other day, my mother asked me to reincarnate her as my child. She wants to be reborn as my daughter. Sometimes, I think of what it would be like to be reborn as someone else, in a different space and time.

There are moments when my mother looks at me and I can see that I am her sun. I illuminate her entire world. Other times, I am the moon. I hide in the safety of shadows, a place where only the darkness is watching. And I reveal myself in phases to her.

Her passion, sometimes, smothers me. Her love and her feelings and her requests, often overwhelm me. Sometimes, I struggle for air, my hands reaching out towards the sky, dancing in distress, silent screams seep like a fog from between my teeth, down my chin, under my jaw, and gather at my neck - and she just refuses to let go until she feels pain in *her* fingers, loses power in *her* wrists.

Chapter 8

Even fire needs to breathe.

I tell this to myself whenever I feel like I've lost love.

Love is a fire – it radiates from the soul. The heart is its furnace – fiery and full of precious metals. Golden smiles. Silver laughter. Copper kisses. Steel strength. So, when love leaves me – by mistake or purposely, I remind myself.

Even fire needs to breathe.

And when I can't find you, I search for you within me.
Are your flames still burning?
Have you taken the time to breathe?
Are you hiding behind my reflection?

Is that you?

Making your presence known in the crackling of my laughter?

When I fail, and am impatient with myself,

Are you the hope that pushes me to try once more?

I could tell you about lost love. I could write an entire book about the pain caused by men who were too afraid, too weak for my heart. I could list their names, their infractions. I could detail the beauty and the beast that I saw living inside of each one of them.

Or, I could gently remind myself that all of the love I ever gave to anyone was a love that I first gave to myself. And that the love I gave to myself was an heirloom gifted to me from the torches of my ancestors and their ancestors – their fire is my internal flame. Never, should I doubt such a truth.

And that each wildfire that blazed through the forests of my heart began from a spark within myself that will never die. It may fade. It may grow quiet and dim. But, it never dies. And I will pass this fire, these flames into the hearts of my children, their children. And even though I may not always feel the scorch of my embers that is simply a sign that I need to take a deep breath. Sometimes, even fire needs to breathe.

www.ingramcontent.com/pod-product-compliance
Lightning Source LLC
Chambersburg PA
CBHW050919160426
43194CB00011B/2469